GOING METRIC

DISCARD

An AMA Survey Report

Alex Groner

George A.W. Boehm

A DIVISION OF AMERICAN MANAGEMENT ASSOCIATIONS

About the Authors

ALEX GRONER received his undergraduate degree in literature from Western Reserve University, and later attended the School of Engineering at the University of Illinois and the Cleveland-Marshall Law School, from which he received a J.D. degree. Although he is a member of the Ohio bar, Mr. Groner decided his interests lay elsewhere than the practice of law. He has worked as a newspaperman for the *Cleveland Press,* as a writer for *Time* magazine, and as manager of internal communications for Time Inc. Since 1967 he has headed Alex Groner Writing Services, Inc., a firm that specializes in corporate and institutional journalism.

In addition to co-authoring *Science in the Service of Mankind,* a history of the Battelle Memorial Institute, Mr. Groner has written the recently published *History of American Business and Industry.*

GEORGE A. W. BOEHM received his undergraduate and graduate training in mathematics at Columbia University. He worked as an editor on *Newsweek, Control Engineering,* and *Scientific American* magazines, then became science–technology editor for *Fortune* for almost ten years. Since 1966 he has been a free-lance writer in New York.

In addition to contributing to many publications, including *The Reader's Digest* and the *New York Times Magazine,* Mr. Boehm authored *The New World of Math,* a semipopular, philosophic exposition of mathematics that has been translated into seven languages. He was one of the writers of *A Metric America,* the book summarizing the U.S. Metric Study of 1968–1971. He and Alex Groner have collaborated before on several projects, including *Science in the Service of Mankind.*

Basis of the Research

Material for this survey report was gathered principally from a questionnaire survey addressed to 5,500 U.S. businessmen. The questionnaires (one questionnaire to a company) were directed primarily to production and engineering managers. The survey was conducted during March and April of 1973, and generated 1,026 usable replies.

The questionnaire was six pages long and included 41 questions; 31 were multiple-choice and the rest were yes–no. The questions covered the use of metric measurements by the respondent companies, the respondents' familiarity and experience with metric, and their personal opinions regarding metrication.

The research effort was rounded out by personal interviews with a number of U.S. businessmen, government officials, and representatives of countries that have recently gone metric or are doing so now.

Contents

1
Highlights
and Conclusions

Major changes that involve legislative action and affect large numbers of people are usually preceded by long gestation periods. An idea may be tossed about for years or even many decades. So it was with the abolition of slavery, the graduated income tax, antitrust laws, and countless other laws with sweeping social and financial implications. In retrospect, all seem inevitable. Nevertheless, they all passed through many phases of controversy, delay, and modification until they were finally accepted.

Another broad change is now in the offing. For the last few years the United States has been seriously contemplating adoption of a simplified and standardized system of weights and measures: the *Système internationale d'unites* (usually called SI). The idea that our nation should adopt uniform measurements in commerce, industry, government, and everyday life is anything but new. In fact, since attempts to legislate such a system date back to the earliest days of the Republic, it is probably the oldest piece of unfinished business in U.S. history.

Today, however, the pressure to "go metric" is much stronger than ever before. Metric is the common language of measurement throughout the world, in all but a handful of tiny, nonindustrial countries. There are, to be sure, several slightly different versions of the metric system. For most purposes the differences are unimportant and cause little or no confusion. Still, in science and advanced technology, where it is essential to speak and write unambiguously, minor discrepancies can cause major problems. Thus, the already-metric nations of the world are converging on SI as a universal language of measurement. It is hardly conceivable that the United States, in converting to metric, would choose any version other than SI.

SI has many demonstrable advantages over the customary U.S. system. Our current measurement language is cluttered with a hodgepodge of special terms, such as therms, rods, and face cords as well as the familiar inches, pounds, and gallons. In contrast, SI has only six basic measurement units and is therefore inherently simpler to learn and use.

As it is, the United States already uses SI to a considerable extent and is gradually drifting toward much greater use of the system. U.S. companies with extensive business abroad often have to use SI in dealing with customers and suppliers. International standards are now being promulgated almost exclusively in SI units, and there is reason to fear that U.S. products that do not conform will be increasingly difficult to export.

DRIFT OR DECISION?

The main procedural question now is whether the United States will continue to drift toward the use of metric or whether it will adopt a deliberate conversion program, coordinated nationwide so that at the end of a specified period SI will be the predominant (though not exclusive) measurement language in use throughout the country.

Since 1971, more than a dozen metric conversion bills have been introduced in Congress. One was actually passed by the Senate in 1972 with virtually no opposition, although it was never brought to a vote in the House. The various bills differ in detail but not in their essential provisions. Briefly, they call for a transition period of ten years, beginning with two years of planning so that businesses and branches of government can dovetail their actions. Participation by firms and individuals will be voluntary. Some may elect to convert in less than five years; others may decide to take considerably longer than ten years; still others may choose not to convert at all. Advisory boards will be set up to coordinate plans. These boards will not have any powers to enforce conversion, but they will provide advice on problems and act as clearinghouses for information.

The success of such a conversion program would depend mainly on those chiefly responsible for carrying it out—namely, U.S. management in all fields of private and public endeavor. This report will concentrate on the former—that is, on managers employed in business and industry. Do these key people really favor conversion? Can they adequately prepare for the task? Are they likely to encounter insuperable problems or ruinous costs along the way?

WHAT THE SURVEY SHOWED

This AMA survey was conducted to determine U.S. management's current attitudes and state of preparedness. More than 1,000 executives responded to a detailed questionnaire, and more than one-third of these supplemented their answers by volunteering comments. In addition, the authors interviewed representatives of several firms that are earnestly planning for metric conversion or have actually begun the changeover without waiting for Congress to act.

In general, the responses to the questionnaire strongly suggest that U.S. commerce and industry are both willing and able to begin an effective conversion program on short notice. Some of the crucial findings are as follows:

- More than three-quarters of the respondents favored a national conversion program.
- More than 80% estimated that a ten-year transition period would be ample.
- More than 75% of the respondents thought it important that their organizations conform to international engineering standards.

- More than 50% now purchase goods abroad. Of these, most were not worried about the possibility that metric conversion by the United States would lead to a flood of imports from nations already familiar with metric.
- Not surprisingly, those respondents who are already conversant with the metric system tend to believe that conversion problems will be minimal.
- Still, about two-thirds of all respondents anticipated significant problems in the area of production during the conversion period.
- Almost half foresaw problems in purchasing and design.
- Fewer than 25% expected difficulties in sales, marketing, clerical work, executive management, packaging, finance, distribution, and legal affairs.
- Only 10% of the respondents said that their organizations have plans for employee education and training, and 59% stated they needed help with this problem.
- Slightly more than half wanted subsidies or tax relief during the conversion period. About one-quarter thought that some legal standards, such as building codes, should be temporarily relaxed.
- Almost 30% wanted advice on explaining their conversion plans to customers or suppliers (a service that coordinating boards are intended to supply).

The experience of the few companies that are already pioneering in metric conversion is heartening. As expected, all are having problems, but in general the problems are much less severe than had been anticipated.

Most of these independent conversion programs are being carried out by a small number of large companies heavily involved in international trade. But their plans are beginning to exert an enormous multiplier force on the movement toward metric. General Motors alone has some 40,000 suppliers, a large number of whom can hardly avoid converting at least partially as GM goes metric with its new products.

APPLYING
THE RULE
OF REASON

The key to relatively cheap and painless conversion seems to be the so-called "rule of reason." This term, used by Lewis Branscomb, former head of the National Bureau of Standards and now an IBM vice president, simply means the budgeting of total transition time so as to avoid costly and disruptive crash programs. According to Branscomb, "Going metric is not really something the federal government can do for the country. People and companies will have to make the changes themselves, at their own pace, and in their own ways."

In the experience of companies that have been converting, almost no production machinery need be scrapped. Most machines can be readily adapted to produce metrically; the rest can be used for the nonmetric products that will be needed until conversion is complete or until they wear out or become obsolete.

The same rule of reason applies to the education and training of workers. For most personnel, a general explanation of company plans in a bulletin or house organ is sufficient. Although a few firms have thought of explaining the entire metric system through films, lectures, and brochures, this kind of costly effort seems more confusing than enlightening. It is far more effective to teach each worker just what he needs to know to do his job, and to postpone training him until just before he needs to know it. A machine, for example, does not really have to know that a kilometer is approximately 5/8 of a mile, that a gram is about 1/30 of an ounce, or that a hectare is 10,000 square meters.

Although many firms and individuals have expressed dread of the expense of metric conversion, costs of well-planned conversions have turned out to be almost insignificant. To be sure, companies are bound to incur expenses in adapting machinery, training workers, and altering drawings and other technical documents. And for a time, during the transition period, companies will be burdened by extra inventories of metric and nonmetric parts. But companies engaged in conversion expect to recoup these costs within a few years—perhaps even before conversion is complete—because it will be simpler and cheaper to do business with one measurement system and because in most cases parts inventories will eventually be reduced far below today's levels.

Experience has shown that the cheapest route to metric is to avoid preliminary studies of possible costs, which are likely to be unrealistic as well as expensive. The most successful strategy, both in the States and in other countries that have been converting, is first to decide to make the change and then to consider, step by step, the most effective ways to minimize costs.

IN THE AFTERMATH OF THE U.S. METRIC STUDY

To a large extent, this AMA survey bears out the U.S. Metric Study, which was carried out by the National Bureau of Standards at the behest of Congress and completed in 1971.* For its time, it was a competent study that led to reasonable conclusions.

Nevertheless, the U.S. Metric Study must now be regarded not as the final word but more as a necessary prelude to further evaluation of metric conversion's problems and opportunities. At the time the NBS began gathering data and soliciting opinions back in 1968, metric conversion was hardly an issue to be viewed seriously in the United States. It is clear that many of those consulted by the NBS had given little or no thought to changing measurement systems. Some companies presented reports in which they confused one metric unit with another. Others envisioned that a conversion program would involve tearing down serviceable buildings in order to replace them with structures designed with metric modules. More than 100 companies were asked to make careful cost studies, but the results were so erratic as to be virtually meaningless. For example, in several cases two companies that were about the same size and produced roughly the same products came up with estimates that differed by a ratio of 10:1 or more.

Since the U.S. Metric Study was begun, and especially since the results were published in a simple book, the idea of a planned and coordinated conversion has passed through the necessary period of gestation. Many people—particularly executives who feel a changeover is inevitable in their company—have had the motivation and the opportunity to ponder most aspects of conversion. Others have had considerable actual experience in planning and carrying out the change to metric. Since we have consulted some of these managers, as well as a broad sample of American businessmen, this survey report can be considered the first exploration of enlightened opinion on the subject.

*The study is summarized in book form in *A Metric America: A Decision Whose Time Has Come,* Report to the Congress. Washington, D.C.: U.S. Government Printing Office, July 1971.

4

2
The Metric System in the United States: Search for a Simple Language

Since the early days of our Republic, the metric system has been advancing into U.S. industry and commerce as irresistibly as a glacier, though not much faster. At this writing, with national metric conversion legislation still pending, the United States finds itself a lonely island in a world that has almost totally abandoned inches and pounds.

Ironically, though, if the second Congress had acted promptly back in 1790, this country would have been the one to introduce a decimal measurement system that other major nations would probably have adopted. The time was ripe for discarding tradition and taking fresh approaches to old problems that had, in the past, been solved haphazardly if at all. Along with a written Constitution, then revolutionary in its concepts, the new nation had adopted a simplified currency. It had discarded the cumbersome English system of pounds, shillings, and pence (as well as such other denominations as guineas, florins, crowns, and farthings). They had been replaced with dollars and cents, which, because of their simple decimal relationship, made computation much easier.

It was in that year that President Washington decided to prepare a new system of weights and measures for Congress to consider, following a Constitutional mandate. He assigned the task to his secretary of state, Thomas Jefferson, an accomplished scientist, engineer, and philosopher. Soon Jefferson came up with a fresh approach: a measurement system based on a natural phenomenon that could be duplicated anywhere in the world. From this phenomenon could be derived all other basic units, conveniently related to each other by multiples of 10, 100, 1,000, and corresponding decimal fractions.

5

The critical basic phenomenon that Jefferson chose was a pendulum that swung to and fro once every two seconds. Its length (actually about 58.7 regular inches) would be subdivided into five "new feet," and each new foot would be further divided into ten "new inches." By using these lengths, plus the specific gravity of pure water, Jefferson was able to derive a complete, consistent, and wholly decimal system of weights and measures. After several lengthy debates and despite repeated proddings by Washington, Congress took no action.

THE FRENCH MOVE AHEAD

Meanwhile, the same antitraditionalist fervor had seized France during the early stages of its revolution. A scientific commission appointed by Talleyrand adopted an approach to measurement that was similar to Jefferson's. Instead of the swing of a pendulum, the commission chose to base its system on a specific fraction of the earth's circumference, determined by a painstaking survey along a meridian running through France. From this fractional length, called the meter, they derived other weights and measures, all related decimally.

In its essential simplicity and reproducibility, the new metric system was little different from Jefferson's scheme. But whereas the U.S. Congress had dallied, the French government adopted the new weights and measures immediately. During the nineteenth century most other major nations converted to the metric system, the few notable exceptions being the British Empire, the United States, and Japan.

In 1816 John Quincy Adams, then secretary of state, was instructed to study again the possibility of adopting a national, standardized system of measurements. In his report he extolled the merits of the metric system and emphasized the advantages of having uniform weights and measures. But he was loath to recommend immediate conversion to metric, because most of the nation's trade was with the adamantly nonmetric British Empire.

Through the rest of the century, the adoption of the metric system was debated sporadically—and often heatedly—in Congress, but no decision was reached. Shortly after the Civil War, bills were passed making metric weights and measures a legal alternative to the customary inch–pound system. And a few years later, the United States became one of the signatories of the Treaty of the Meter, which refined and standardized the units of the metric system.

Finally, in 1893, the United States became *officially* a metric country. The secretary of the treasury proclaimed that the meter bar and kilogram weight were the fundamental legal standards, while the yard, the pound, and other, more familiar units were redefined as fractions or multiples of the metric units.

The immediate impact of this change was negligible outside a few fields of science and engineering. Congress, sometimes by narrow margins, defeated several bills that would have propelled metric conversion in commerce, industry, and everyday life.

But as the world shrank, as trade with metric nations increased, and as two world wars were fought with metric nations as allies, the question of metric conversion became steadily more pressing. In 1957 the U.S. army established the metric system as a standard for weapons and related equipment. In 1960 a U.S. delegation participated in a conference that further refined metric measurements and reached agreement on more precise standards, which were needed especially for high-precision work in science and technology. These standards, known collectively as *Système internationale d'unites* (popularly called SI), serve as the King's English of metric systems.

THE BRITISH
CHANGEOVER

But in spite of its advantages, the metric system was, as late as 1960, little closer to being the common measurement system of the United States than it had been in John Quincy Adams' day. Then almost overnight came a forced change in official attitudes. The United Kingdom, through its Board of Trade, announced that it intended to adopt the metric system over a course of ten years, beginning in 1965. The rest of the Commonwealth nations prepared to follow suit. Since Japan had, after much backing and filling, finally converted to metric in the early 1960s, the United States faced the prospect of using measurements that the rest of the industrial world could understand only with difficulty.

THE U.S.
RESPONSE

Congress responded in 1968 by authorizing the Commerce Department to make a three-year study of all the questions relating to U.S. metric conversion in the near future. How could it best be accomplished? What would be the costs and benefits? How far should the federal government go in encouraging or dictating conversion?

The results of this study, published in the summer of 1971, were highly favorable to advocates of metric conversion. In brief, the report endorsing something like the British ten-year plan, with all sectors of society participating voluntarily and moving at their own pace. Aside from eventually adopting metric standards in its dealing with business and consumers, the government would do little more than appoint and finance coordinating and planning boards, which would be disbanded as soon as conversion had been nearly completed. People who preferred to stick with the old, familiar measurements would be free to do so. For example, wood could still be sold by the cord; printers could speak of points and picas; the height of a racehorse might still be expressed in hands; and housewives could continue to order a pound of butter (although in time they would get half a kilogram, which is just a little more than a pound).

Planned and programmed evolution, rather than revolution, was the theme of the U.S. Metric Study. It urged a ten-year transition, including a preliminary planning stage of about two years. In 1972 bills embodying this spirit were introduced in both houses of Congress. The Senate version passed with virtually no opposition, but the House failed to bring its bill to a vote.

Similar bills have been introduced in 1973. Experienced "Congress watchers" expect little or no opposition, although it may take some time to settle details. And so, as the nation approaches its bicentennial, Jefferson's fundamental ideas may at last be adopted by his own countrymen.

3
The World
and Metric Systems

When the Senate passed its metric conversion bill in 1972, both *The New York Times* and *The New Yorker* magazine denounced the proposed legislation as a nonlaw. These publications, usually staunch proponents of individual initiative, wanted a bill with teeth that would make the changeover mandatory and swift.

The same attitude was expressed by a small minority of the participants in the U.S. Metric Study. They would prefer to outlaw, as soon as possible, the use of nonmetric units in industry, commerce, and everyday life.

If this all-out program were to be adopted (and if it could be enforced), the United States would become the only *completely* metric nation on earth. History shows that all measurement systems, including metric, behave like languages: they are constantly evolving. Old units, such as the cubit and the ell, are abandoned. New ones are added when necessary, as when the development of electricity called for precise definitions of the volt, the ampere, the ohm, and so forth.

Moreover, even in metric nations, a certain amount of measurement "slang" persists and is indeed useful for special purposes. Astronomers the world over still speak of "light years" and "parsecs" instead of trillions of kilometers. It is most convenient for meteorologists to adhere to "bars" and "millibars," one bar being roughly equal to normal atmospheric pressure. The U.S. football field will continue to be 100 yards long, and no one will try to express this length as 91.44 meters. Even in France, the birthplace of the metric system, many shoppers still order groceries by the *livre* (the old French pound). They get half a kilogram, slightly more than a pound, but the discrepancy bothers no one but purists. And in all other metric countries handy old units persist and will probably never die out of the language of measurement. The metric system itself sticks with the traditional, nondecimal division of time—60 seconds to the minute, 60 minutes to the hour, and 24 hours to the day. In every nation and every occupation, some nonmetric units will continue to be useful and widely used.

For most people, tables of decimal prefixes and of common conversion factors will suffice for everyday usage. (See Exhibits 1 and 2.)

EXHIBIT 1. Meaning and Use of Metric Prefixes

Prefix	Meaning	Use
tera	A trillion times (10^{12})	By scientists and technicians
giga	A billion times (10^9)	By scientists and technicians
mega	A million times (10^6)	Fairly common
kilo	A thousand times (10^3)	Quite common
hecto	A hundred times (10^2)	Rare
deca	Ten times (10)	Rare
deci	A tenth (10^{-1})	Rare
centi	A hundredth (10^{-2})	Quite common
milli	A thousandth (10^{-3})	Quite common
micro	A millionth (10^{-6})	Quite common
nano	A billionth (10^{-9})	By scientists and technicians
pico	A trillionth (10^{-12})	By scientists and technicians

EXHIBIT 2. Some Quick Conversions

	If you know:	You can get:	If you multiply by*:
Length	inches	millimeters	25
	feet	centimeters	30
	yards	meters	0.9
	miles	kilometers	1.6
	millimeters	inches	0.04
	centimeters	inches	0.4
	meters	yards	1.1
	kilometers	miles	0.6
Area	square inches	square centimeters	6.5
	square feet	square meters	0.09
	square yards	square meters	0.8
	square miles	square kilometers	2.6
	acres	square hectometers (hectares)	0.4
	square centimeters	square inches	0.16
	square meters	square yards	1.2
	square kilometers	square miles	0.4
	square hectometers	acres	2.5
Mass (and weight)	ounces	grams	28
	pounds	kilograms	0.45
	short tons	megagrams (metric tons)	0.9
	grams	ounces	0.035
	kilograms	pounds	2.2
	megagrams (metric tons)	short tons	1.1
Liquid volume	ounces	milliliters	30
	pints	liters	0.47
	quarts	liters	0.95
	gallons	liters	3.8
	milliliters	ounces	0.034
	liters	pints	2.1
	liters	quarts	1.06
	liters	gallons	0.26
Temperature	degrees Fahrenheit	degrees Celsius	5/9 (after subtracting 32)
	degrees Celsius	degrees Fahrenheit	9/5 (and then add 32)

*The conversion factors are all approximate, but close enough to be useful for all practical purposes. The greater the degree of precision desired, the less "quick" the conversions are likely to be.

**SI: WHERE
PURISM COUNTS**

In some areas, nevertheless, metric purism plays a vital role. This is particularly true in definitions of engineering standards. Certainly a purist approach to measurement is imperative whenever precise agreement on standards can make a difference between life and death. It is also imperative when the issue is whether a product will be accepted or rejected in foreign markets.

The general public and even most sophisticated businessmen hardly realize how many areas engineering standards cover. It is taken for granted that a hardware store can supply a standard nut to fit a standard bolt. But the importance of engineering standards should not be overlooked: These standards serve as both a dictionary and a recipe book for a technical society. They can be applied, for example, to all of the following: the diameter of copper wire and the composition and thickness of its insulation; the purity of aspirin; the water content of a ham; a laboratory method to test the sulphur content of fuel oil; the fire resistance of a child's nightgown; many details in local building codes; the wattage of a toaster; the weight of a dime; the size and shape of highway signs and their symbols.

The International Standards Organization (ISO), which is promulgating worldwide engineering standards, has settled on SI as a desirable measurement language. Metric purists decry the continuing use of measurement units that are not strictly according to SI. A few even despise the use of "liter," a measure of volume slightly larger than the U.S. quart. They point out that in SI it is correctly called a cubic deciliter. But since the deciliter is one metric unit almost never used in common parlance, the now familiar liter will probably never disappear from the language of measurement.

Thus, for almost all purposes it is enough for a nation to adhere *predominantly* to SI. Any attempt to make people apply the metric system to every aspect of their daily lives is likely to be as futile as trying to convert the world to Esperanto or one of the other synthetic languages that have been proposed.

SI is based on only six measurement units. The basic length is the meter. The basic weight is the kilogram. The unit of time is the second. Electric current is measured in amperes. The temperature scale is Kelvin, although for most purposes Celsius (formerly called Centigrade) is acceptable. And luminous intensity is expressed in candela. From these units others can be derived, including those for force, energy, pressure, and electric power. All the derived units have simple decimal relationships. None are so computationally clumsy as customary U.S. measures (e.g., the horsepower, which equals 550 foot-pounds per second).

The immense task of establishing all international engineering standards that the world will need has hardly begun. So far, ISO and its electrical counterpart, the International Electrotechnical Commission (IEC), have agreed on about 3,000 standards. The goal is roughly 10,000 by the end of this decade, and by the end of the century technological advances may compel many more additions and revisions.

**ANSI's
ROLE IN
STANDARDIZATION**

The U.S. representative at ISO and IEC deliberations is the American National Standards Institute (ANSI), an organization sponsored and supported by business and industry. Although ANSI delegates are well versed in SI, they are encountering some difficulty in getting their views accepted because U.S. national standards are often in the old inch–pound system. Meanwhile, small nations, lacking strong standards bodies of their own, are tending more and more to accept ISO and IEC standards without question.

One of the strongest arguments for metric conversion is that it would enhance U.S. influence in international standards-making and thus increase the likelihood that U.S. technological ideas would be adopted by other nations. For this reason, ANSI has spoken out strongly for a prompt and orderly conversion to the metric system.

ANSI has even gone so far as to appoint an American National Metric Council. Its 22-person executive committee, headed by Adrian G. Weaver, IBM's director of standards practices, includes representatives from labor, education, home-economics, and engineering societies as well as the small and large businesses that are the backbone of ANSI's membership.

Thus, the nation already has a framework of technical experts who are well acquainted with the most important problems and opportunities. This will simplify matters when and if Congress decides to press ahead with metric conversion.

Virtually all technical people agree that worldwide engineering standards represent a worthwhile goal that will inevitably be approached in years to come. They agree also that the vast majority of standards will be based on the metric system. That is to say, if a certain part has been standardized in the United States to be ½ inch in diameter (12.7 millimeters), a corresponding international standard will call for either a 12-millimeter or a 13-millimeter diameter.

SOME HOLDOUTS

Still, international engineering standards are likely to remain a mixture of metric units and inch–pound units. Metric countries use small pipes with metric diameters, but because oil pipeline technology was developed mainly in the United States, very large pipes are still measured in feet and inches and are unlikely to be changed soon, if ever. Ordinary camera film is made to bastard specifications (35 millimeters wide, with 6 sprocket holes to the inch). A redesign would enrage millions of photographers the world over, although new camera models designed for purely metric film might over the course of many years make current film obsolete.

In a few areas, agreement on worldwide standards is unlikely ever to be reached. As travelers well know, such electrical appliances as American-made electric razors do not work on European current. The reason is that household current throughout Europe is distributed at 220 volts, 50 hertz (cycles per second), whereas the U.S. standard is 115 volts, 60 hertz. But then, as in the case of non-metric "slang" terms, the world can afford some deviations from rigid and universal standardization.

DECIMAL DIVIDENDS OF THE METRIC SYSTEM

Advocates of measurement conversion stress that the metric system is completely harmonious with ordinary decimal arithmetic and therefore much more convenient to use. In fact, engineers who have made detailed studies estimate that the design and drafting departments of very large companies may save hundreds of thousands of dollars per year through time saved on manual computations (i.e., computations done with a desk calculator, a slide rule, or paper and pencil).

In the customary inch–pound system, for example, they must grapple with such awkward operations as dividing by 778 to convert foot-pounds to a different energy unit (the British thermal unit), or multiplying by 231 to change gallons into cubic inches. Such arithmetic manipulations not only consume time but also increase the chance of error. Similar metric conversions, in contrast, usually involve no more than moving a decimal point.

It is only fair, however, to note that decimal arithmetic has already made inroads into many practical applications of the inch–pound system. Highway signs (and automobile odometers) usually give fractions of miles in tenths, rather than in some clumsy number of yards or feet. And since long before World War II, precision parts have been machined and gauged to hundredths, thousandths, and even ten-thousandths of an inch.

Incidentally, rash statements that the metric system is more accurate because it is decimal are unfounded. Accuracy depends entirely on the quality of measurement tools and the skill of the men who use them.

METRIC CONVERSION IN OTHER COUNTRIES

If and when the United States decides to launch a metric conversion program, history furnishes a wealth of precedents. Every nation that has deliberately gone metric has proceeded in its own way. And although none can furnish a flawless blueprint for the United States, many good ideas could be adopted and many outright blunders avoided.

Perhaps the worst-conceived metric conversion program in history was the first. In 1795, while still beset by war and revolutionary upheavals, the French government abruptly decreed that the new system of weights and measures must be adopted immediately.

Instantaneous and mandatory conversion did little but add to the chaos of the times. The manufacture and distribution of standard meters and kilograms lagged. Finally in 1882, to allay confusion, Napoleon partially reinstated traditional weights and measures, while retaining the metric system as an almost theoretical standard. Not until 1837, when Napoleon's decree was repealed, did France commit itself again to full metric conversion. Thus, ironically, the only nation that has ever adopted the metric system and then abandoned it was the metric mother country.

Another example of confusion compounded by delay is the Japanese experience. Conversion could have been relatively simple, for it began in 1921, before Japan emerged as a great industrial power. At that time the country had three officially recognized measurement systems: metric, British, and a traditional system based on the *shaku* (slightly less than 1 foot) and the *kan* (about 8¼ pounds).

The Japanese Diet passed a law to phase out the British and traditional systems. Primary schools, government agencies, public utilities, and a few other key industries were to become wholly metric within ten years. The rest of the economy was allowed twenty years to make the change. But this plan was balked and disrupted by, in turn, the Great Depression, a surge of chauvinism, a disastrous war, and military occupation by a power committed to the inch–pound system.

12

Not until 1951 did Japan again set its sights on becoming a metric nation. Although the new target date of 1958 was not met, conversion was mostly completed by the early 1960s. Like the children of Israel en route to the Promised Land, the Japanese had wandered for forty years toward the adoption of the metric system.

The conversion plan most often cited as a possible model for the United States is Britain's current "metrication" program. As late as 1960 a joint committee of the British Association for the Advancement of Science and the Association of British Chambers of Commerce made an industrial survey. The conclusion was that metrication would be premature, because the United States and most of the Commonwealth, Britain's chief trading partners, were still committed to inches and pounds. Just three years later, however, the British Standards Institution made a similar survey and learned that a large majority of firms favored starting metrication as soon as possible.

Industry took the initiative. In 1965 the president of the Federation of British Industries asked the government (then Labour) to accept nationwide metrication over a ten-year period. The government conceded that the change was desirable and, while leaving industry in charge, agreed to adjust its procurement policies in step with progress of the program.

A two-year planning stage began immediately under a Metrication Board that represented distributors, retailers, educational institutions, and the general public, as well as industry. From the beginning it was agreed that the board would have no power to coerce an industry or company to convert and that the government would do nothing to offset the costs of metrication. Exhibit 3 shows the conversion schedules for industries (left) and for industrial products and materials (right).

The metrication program started ambitiously with early conversion of the construction industry, which has interfaces with a great many diverse manufacturers and also employs an enormous variety of skilled and unskilled labor. This daring move worked well. By the end of 1972, almost all materials, from bolts to bricks, were available in standard metric sizes and most new construction was designed to metric modules. In order to ease conversion, the British construction industry decided to favor a basic module of 300 millimeters, an odd size but one that is conveniently familiar because it is almost exactly equal to one foot.

On the whole, British metrication has proceeded smoothly enough. But it will miss its 1975 target date by at least two years, and consumers will probably not become fully acclimated until 1980. The lag can be traced largely to a loss of momentum in 1971, when Parliament was debating joining the Common Market and the government was preparing a long-awaited white paper, delineating its views on metrication. The reason for procrastination vanished when Britain did indeed join the Common Market and when the white paper guardedly endorsed metrication, though warning that the government "will not, however, use public purchasing power deliberately to hasten the changeover from imperial to metric units." A few industries are still hampered in their conversion efforts by the Weights and Measures Act of 1963, which specifies imperial units and has not yet been amended.

13

EXHIBIT 3.   British Timetable for Industrial Metrication Programs

General programmes	1969	1970	1971	1972	1973	1974	1975

Construction industry

Metric standards							
Metric products & materials							
Metric design							
Metric construction							

Electrical industry

Metric standards							
Metric products & materials							
Metric design							
Metric production							

Marine industry

Metric standards							
Metric products & materials							
Metric design							
Metric construction							

Engineering industries

Metric standards							
Metric products & materials							
Metric design							
Metric production							

Legend

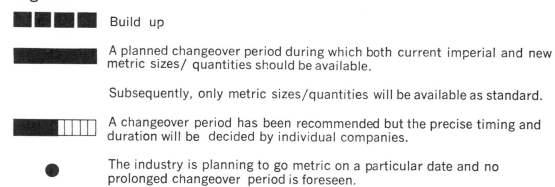

Build up

A planned changeover period during which both current imperial and new metric sizes/ quantities should be available.

Subsequently, only metric sizes/quantities will be available as standard.

A changeover period has been recommended but the precise timing and duration will be decided by individual companies.

The industry is planning to go metric on a particular date and no prolonged changeover period is foreseen.

14

Commodity	1969	1970	1971	1972
Adhesives		●		
Aluminum: castings		▬		
Aluminum: foil		▬		
Aluminum: wrought		▬		
Asphalt			▬▭	▭
Ball and roller bearings	▬▬▬	▬▬	▭	
Blockboard		▬		
Board: insulating	●			
Board: paper			●	
Board: pasted display and showcard			●	
Board: printing			●	
Boxes: crates etc.		●		
Boxes: metal			▬	
Bricks		▬▭		
Building blocks	▬▬	▭		
Cables		●		
Cellulose film		▬		
Cement			●	
Chemicals general: in all trade in the U.K.	▬▬▬	▬▬	▭▭	
Chemicals general: in trade between member firms	▬▬	▭▭		
Clay		▬▭		
Concrete pipes			▬	▭
Copper and copper alloy: wire rod, sheet, strip etc.		▬▭		
Expanded polystyrene board		▬		
Fasteners	▬▬▬	▬▬	▭	
Fibre board packing cases		●		
Glass: flat	▬▬	▬		
Hides and skins: unprocessed		●		
Paint			▬	
Paper: blotting			●	
Paper: book printing		●		
Paper: cover			●	
Paper: machine glazed for envelopes and posters			●	

Commodity	1969	1970	1971	1972
Paper: manilla		●		
Paper: printing and writing		●		
Paper: specialty coated		●		
Paper: waterproof		▬		
Paper: wrapping	●			
Paving flags		▬▭		
Pesticides				▭▭
Pharmaceutical	▬			
Photographic equipment	▬▬▬	▬▬	▬▭	▭
Photographic materials		▬▬	▬▬	▬
Pitch fibre pipes	●			
Plaster			●	
Plaster-board		▬		
Plywood: home produced		●		
Plywood: imported	●			
Polythene: film		●		
Polypropylene; film		▬		
PVC: calendered rigid		▬		
PVC: extruded film		▬		
Ready-mixed concrete			●	
Roofing felt		▬		
Sand and gravel				▭▭
Scientific and industrial instruments	▬▬▬	▬▬	▬▭	▭
Slag		▬▬	▬	▭
Steel bars and mesh for concrete reinforcement	▬			
Stone and chalk			▬	▭
Synthetic rubber		▬▭		
Textile fibres for commercial users: wool, cotton, jute, synthetic			●	
Timber: home grown		●		
Timber: imported		▬		
Windows: aluminum	▬▬	▬		
Windows: steel			▬▬	▬
Wire: insulated		▬▬	▭	
Wood pulp	●			

Source: This exhibit is reproduced from *A Metric America: A Decision Whose Time Has Come*. Washington, D.C.: U.S. Government Printing Office, July 1971.

EXHIBIT 4. Australian Postage Stamps

When the U.S. House of Representatives Committee on Science and Astronautics held metric conversion hearings in May 1973, it got a revealing summary of British metrication from a visiting expert, Lord Ritchie-Calder, who was the original chairman of the Metrication Board. He concluded his account as follows:

> The lessons of metrication for me are quite simple. That it is not only desirable but inevitable; those who do not come in will be out in the cold. It is, in terms of increased efficiency and profitability, good business. The problems are complex at first sight but reasonably simple when they are broken down into sectors and components. Training is a non-problem. . . . Experience has shown that training should be limited to the minimum necessary and given only when the workers are embarking immediately on metric units. . . . One of the most important lessons is that it pays dividends to keep the actual period of change as short as practicable.

If the British could retrace their steps, they would probably begin with a stratagem adopted by the Australian Metric Conversion Board. Australia's problems were simpler, mainly because the nation is not so heavily industrialized and also because, by the time planning began in 1970, the board could draw on five years of British experience.

However, where the British concentrated their early efforts on industry, the Australians began by educating the general public with a simple 18-page booklet mailed in 1972 to every household in the country. This booklet concentrates on the measurements that people will need in everyday life and encourages them to "think metric" rather than to use conversion tables. This typical paragraph includes some generally useful benchmarks: "A five cent piece is about 1 millimetre thick and a Queen's head stamp is 2 centimetres wide, a metre is a long pace and from Melbourne to Perth is 2500 kilometres, the mass of a 20 cent piece is about 10 grams, . . . 25°C is a pleasantly warm day."

Whereas the British have avoided setting firm dates for complete conversion, the Australians have dramatized their "think metric" program with a series of highly publicized "M days" (and months) on which complete conversion would take place in a particular field. These included October 1971 for wool sales, August 1972 for horse races, and September 1972 for weather news. British television and radio announcers, in contrast, began by announcing the temperature in both Celsius and Fahrenheit degrees, until a study showed that an overwhelming majority of listeners mentally blocked out the Celsius figure and waited impatiently for the Fahrenheit number.

With Australia, South Africa, New Zealand, and most of the other Commonwealth nations converting to metric, the list of countries still committed to inches and pounds is shrinking rapidly. At this writing it consists of Barbados, Burma, Gambia, Jamaica, Liberia, Nauru, Sierra Leone, Tonga, Yemen Arab Republic, Yemen People's Democratic Republic, and the United States of America.

4
How U.S. Business Feels About Metrication

The metric system of measurement, like politics and football, arouses strong partisan feelings in Americans. Of 1,026 respondents to the AMA questionnaire, fully 346 volunteered comments—and only ten of those comments could be regarded as noncommittal.

The opinions offered ranged from the thoughtfully reasoned to the emotionally violent, from the uncompromisingly negative ("Why metric? The English system is beautiful! . . . Next step after metrication of machines and parts could be metrication of you and me. Think about it!") to the impatiently affirmative ("The longer we b——t about it the more it will cost. Let's do it now and philosophize about it later. We didn't grow great by talking about things.")

But overall, a significant majority of respondents (762, or 77%) favor a nation-wide conversion to the metric system, while 23% are opposed to it. Most respondents (81%) feel that the best time frame for such a conversion is between one and ten years, with 42% favoring a one-to-five-year conversion period and 39% preferring a five-to-ten-year period.

The majority of respondents (58%) are more in favor of a nationwide conversion to metric than they were five years earlier. Of the remaining 42%, several pointed out that they could not be *more* in favor, since they were already firmly pro-metric five years ago.

ABOUT THE RESPONDENTS

Approximately half the respondents (511) were in the manufacturing field. The next largest groups were construction (117 respondents) and public utilities (99 respondents). The remaining respondents were distributed as shown in Exhibit 5.

EXHIBIT 5. Measurement Sensitivity of Responding Companies, by Industrial Classification

Industrial Classification	No. of Respondents	Degree of Measurement Sensitivity in Respondents' Companies			
		Great	Moderate	Minimal	Little or None
Manufacturing	511	59%	30%	9%	2%
Construction	117	63	30	6	1
Public utilities	99	58	29	11	2
Transportation	53	37	41	14	8
Finance, Insurance, and Real estate	45	13	9	33	45
Mining	43	30	27	41	2
Services	43	47	24	19	10
Communications	41	35	35	27	3
Retail trade	23	22	47	22	9
Diversified	20	35	45	15	5
Wholesale trade	12	50	17	8	25
Agriculture	7	43	14	43	—
Public administration	4	75	25	—	—
Other	8	43	29	14	14

A third of the companies in the survey reported annual sales of $100 million or more. Only 14% of the firms have more than 10,000 employees; 23% have between 2,000 and 10,000; the rest have fewer than 2,000.

More than half (52%) of the companies said their processes, work procedures, or products were highly "measurement sensitive" (i.e., precise measurements make an important difference to them). Another 30% said their companies were measurement sensitive to a moderate extent, and only 5% reported little or no measurement sensitivity.

Breakdown of measurement sensitivity by industry is given in Exhibit 5. All industries believe themselves to be measurement sensitive to some degree, and even in the Finance, Insurance, and Real estate classification, one-eighth of the respondents felt their organizations were measurement sensitive to a great extent. Of those industry groups for which samples were large enough to be significant, the group that believes itself to be most measurement sensitive is Construction, with 63% of respondents believing their firms to be sensitive to a great extent and another 30% to a moderate extent. This compared with 59% and 30% for Manufacturing, and 58% and 29% for Utilities.

The respondents were also broken down by percentages of technically trained personnel in their companies. These were the results:

22% of responding companies	had	more than 25% technically trained employees
26% of responding companies	had	10–25% technically trained employees
28% of reponding companies	had	5–19% technically trained employees
24% of responding companies	had	fewer than 5% technically trained employees

More than three-fourths of those responding feel it is important that their organizations conform to national and international engineering standards for weights and measures. However, only 11% believe that international agreement on such standards would be likely to cut their production costs by as much as 5%.

Most respondents feel that metric conversion in the United States would do little toward simplifying standardization of products or procedures, with 26% replying it would not at all, 41% hardly at all, 25% to a moderate extent, and only 8% to a great extent.

The predominant opinion was that conversion to metrics would not affect the cost of doing business—73% thought it would not, while 9% believed their costs would increase, 7% thought they would decrease, and the remaining 11% felt they could make no assessment. The longer the conversion period, most respondents believed, the lower their costs would be. In the event of a five-year conversion, 64% thought the costs would be less than 5% of a year's sales; if conversion took ten years, 74% felt costs would be below that level. (See Exhibit 6.)

EXHIBIT 6. Estimated Conversion Costs, as Percentage of Annual Sales

FOR A 5-YEAR CONVERSION PERIOD:		*FOR A 10-YEAR CONVERSION PERIOD:*	
Percent of Companies	*Estimated Cost (Percent of Annual Sales)*	*Percent of Companies*	*Estimated Cost (Percent of Annual Sales)*
64%	Less than 5%	75%	Less than 5%
24	5–10%	18	5–10%
9	11–25%	6	11–25%
3	More than 25%	2	More than 25%

Thirty-five percent of the respondents felt that the cost of adapting machinery and equipment to the metric system would amount to less than 5% of its present value; 15% thought it would be in the 5–10% range, 11% thought it would be 11–25%, and a whopping 39% thought it would amount to more than a fourth of present value.

A total of 217 respondents (22%) said that their companies produce to inch-pound measurements for their U.S. market and to metric measurements for their foreign market. The proportion of goods made to metric measurements ranged from less than 10% to more than 50%. (Of these companies, most—i.e., 134 respondents—fell in the below-10% range, while only 11 respondents fell in the above-50% range.)

Something over half of the respondents (54%) said their companies now purchase goods or supplies from abroad. A similar percentage said they do not believe foreign purchases by U.S. companies would be significantly affected by conversion to the metric system.

Comments and opinions were offered freely by 346 of the respondents. A cross-check of their answers to the question on whether they favored a metric conversion showed them to be for it by a four-to-one margin, as opposed to just a three-to-one edge for all respondents to the questionnaire. About 35 comments urged that the conversion begin as soon as possible, including 10 to the effect that the development was inevitable so "let's get it over with."

Fifty-six commenters said they favored a compulsory or mandatory approach. Twelve thought metrication should be voluntary.

A few advocated some form of subsidization of the costs of metrication. Four called for tax relief or incentive, two for subsidies, two for government purchases to finance the conversion. One simply said that government should ease the financial pain. One commenter said industry can't justify the costs alone; another said industry should bear all the costs. A handful commented that there should be no subsidies, because these would inevitably turn into boondoggles.

A sampling of the respondents' remarks:

- "Having installed a waste water control plan, made extensive capital expenditures to comply with OSHA [the Occupational Safety and Health Act], anticipating major expenditures for air and noise pollution, etc., we wonder how many more regulations can be met before we sink altogether!"
- "When a manufacturer finds out that it will help beat competition, he will convert to metric. . . . When we need to, we'll convert. Let *demand* force it—not the almighty government."
- "Our company is presently converting all labels on packages to show inch-pound and metric measurements, as well as decimal packing."
- "Maximum benefits will not be obtained unless archaic building codes are also standardized along with the conversion."
- "The thing I fear most is a long period of partial conversion. Get it over with."
- "Each year we do more export business, so the sooner we go metric the better."
- ". . . I hate to think what the Communist world could do to the U.S.A. when we would be five years into a ten-year conversion plan. It would be catastrophic."
- "Most proponents of metrication have no knowledge of conversion implications and difficulties, particularly with respect to preferred number systems of standard sizes, as in sheet metal, wire, and screw sizes. Do you realize that a 2″ X 4″ (lumber) becomes 4.13 X 9.21 cm?"
- "Would be great to convert. However, I doubt if it would rid us of: Type size—picas, wood 2 X 4's that are not 2 X 4's, . . . reams of paper, ABC shoe widths."
- ". . . during the conversion the public will be subjected to many inconveniences and possibly additional costs. For example, obtaining spare parts for home appliances, automobiles, etc. . . . Power conversion from 120V to 240V in household appliances and the rewiring of homes . . . will become a major problem. . . ."
- "As my company is involved in food distribution, . . . I feel the metric system would be a fantastic benefit to the retail supermarket operator and even more so to the shopper on computing and comparing prices and values."
- "I believe this to be hogwash. Let the damn Europeans convert to our system."

- "The greatest problem in our industry (engines) will be in manufacturing spare parts in inches and new parts in metric units . . . for perhaps forty or fifty years because of the long life of our product. Nevertheless I am strongly in favor of conversion as completely and as soon as possible."
- "This is the new world—inches and pounds. Why go back to the old world—metric systems?"
- "I trust this questionnaire will prove a valuable *meterstick* in evaluating the transition."

THE CRACKERJACK EFFECT

The observation that the more people use the metric system, the more they like it—what one wag at the Bureau of Standards called "the crackerjack effect"—was borne out in much of the survey.

Familiarity with metrics was inferred from answers to a question about personal grasp of the metric system. More than a third (35%) said they do not use the system at all, and these were judged to be the least familiar; 6% said they use it "with great difficulty," another 35% use it "with some difficulty," and 24% use it "with ease and familiarity." As might be expected, the respondents most familiar with metrics tended to work for companies that produce to metric measurements for the foreign market and that buy goods and services abroad.

The more familiar the respondents were with the metric system, the more they tended to favor it. Sixty percent of the "never use" group favor nationwide conversion, 70% of the "great difficulty" group, 86% of the "some difficulty" group, and 88% of the "ease and familiarity" group.

A similar result was obtained when respondents were asked whether employees who use metric measurements tend to like them. Going up the scale again from least to most familiar groups, the "yes" answers ran 15%, 10%, 15%, and 27%, while the "no" responses were 25%, 30%, 19%, and 13%. In all groups, some 60% felt it made no difference to employees.

Familiarity with metric also appeared to affect respondents' perceptions of the impact of metrication. In general, those more familiar tended to be most optimistic about the ease of using metric, the costs of conversion, and subsequent costs or savings. Too, the most familiar tended to expect fewer difficulties with suppliers and customers in the event of national conversion. The percentages of the least familiar and most familiar groups that expect trouble in various problem areas are shown in Exhibit 7.

As for costs, only 7% of the least familiar group believed production costs would be cut by 5% or more by international agreement on engineering standards, while 19% of the most familiar group professed that belief.

Surprisingly, however, the least familiar did not estimate higher costs of conversion than the most familiar. Given a five-year conversion period, 68% of the "never use" group thought costs would run less than 5% of a year's sales, and 20% thought they would run from 5% to 10%. In the "use with ease and familiarity" group, 60% felt that costs would be under 5% and 27% thought they would amount to 5–10% of a year's sales. Replies were similar with regard to a ten-year conversion period.

EXHIBIT 7. Personal Grasp of the Metric System as a Factor in Judging Anticipated Problems During Conversion

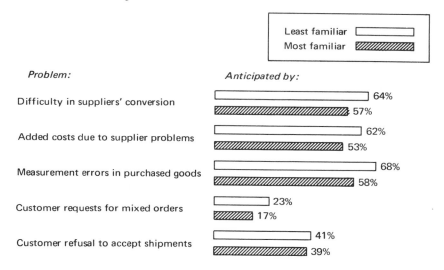

| | Least familiar | ▢ |
| | Most familiar | ▨ |

Problem: Anticipated by:

Difficulty in suppliers' conversion — 64% / 57%

Added costs due to supplier problems — 62% / 53%

Measurement errors in purchased goods — 68% / 58%

Customer requests for mixed orders — 23% / 17%

Customer refusal to accept shipments — 41% / 39%

The great majority in all groups thought the costs of doing business after conversion would remain about the same, but 12% of the least familiar thought costs would go up and 4% thought they would go down, while only 6% of the most familiar expected costs to rise and 12% thought they would drop.

The more familiar respondents also showed much greater confidence that conversion would simplify standardization of products or procedures. Going from least to most familiar, the percentages of the groups believing this would happen "to a great extent" were 4%, 6%, 6%, and 15%, respectively. The percentages believing it would take place "to a moderate extent" were 16%, 37%, 29%, and 31%, respectively. Forty-one percent of the least familiar group felt conversion would not affect standardization at all; only 15% of the most familiar group felt it would have no effect.

U.S. COMPANIES TAKING STEPS TOWARD CONVERSION

Beginning in 1972, several U.S. companies announced plans to begin metric conversion on their own without waiting for national legislation. All are multinationals, which must in any event conduct much of their business in metric language and metric standards. The number is still small, but the impact of their action promises to be great, for included among these pioneers are such giants as Caterpillar Tractor, Deere & Company, Ford Motor, General Motors, Honeywell, IBM, and International Harvester. In addition, several smaller firms that manufacture tools, hardware, and other products used throughout industry are increasing their metric outputs.

In moving toward metric independently, these companies are generally following the path recommended in the U.S. Metric Study. That is to say, metrication is an evolutionary program, not a revolution. When nonmetric machines and procedures wear out, become obsolete, or need replacement for other reasons, the company uses that opportunity to introduce metric products, equipment, and standards. Ideally, nothing that is structurally sound and functional is scrapped merely for the sake of going metric.

The confident, though still limited, shift to metric represents a sharp trend that has become evident only within the last two to three years. In 1970, while the National Bureau of Standards was gathering opinions and data for the U.S. Metric Study, most firms were preoccupied with an economic slump, new pollution regulations, and other problems. Few had given more than fleeting attention to the possibility of changing their weights and measures. Thus it was only natural that many of the responses were, to say the least, erratic.

The precepts of the metric pioneers can do much to allay doubts such as those expressed by Donald L. Peyton, managing director of the American National Standards Institute. Shortly after ANSI set up its Metric Council in fall of 1972, Peyton warned: "One can reasonably deduce that today the United States is far from ready for metric conversion. The real problem is that many of our industrial concerns have not even begun serious planning for metrication. These companies and even whole industries may find themselves in uncharted waters without navigational equipment with which to steer a proper course."

RISING LEVELS OF AWARENESS

Nevertheless, the general level of awareness and sophistication seems to be rising rapidly. In May 1973, for instance, the American Management Associations conducted an intensive two-day briefing on such topics as premature obsolescence of tools, dual inventories, and standardizing dimension systems. The participants were obviously concerned and eager for ideas and information. It was clear that the climate had changed abruptly since three years before, when a favorite wisecrack at the National Bureau of Standards was: "I think metric conversion is perfectly all right, but only among consenting adults."

Some industrial leaders have endorsed a national metric conversion program without announcing specific plans to change their own product lines. At the 1972 Senate hearings, a General Electric representative spoke in favor of the flexible, voluntary, government-coordinated plan recommended in the U.S. Metric Study. But, while it continues to study conversion problems, GE is presumably content to postpone action until Congress passes a bill.

In April 1973 General Motors announced a policy that is generally in accord with the Branscomb rule of reason. The company will switch to metric for all new products, including the Wankel rotary engine and other items now in the development stage. Products now being manufactured will remain as they are—i.e., conforming to what one respondent to this AMA survey called "the automotive industry's own bastard set of standards." Meanwhile, GM will pay special attention to coordinating its changes with its nearly 40,000 suppliers of parts, components, equipment, and services.

Ford has made no such formal commitment, but early in June it opened the first metric engine plant in the United States. An addition to Ford's Lima, Ohio plant, it will manufacture four-cylinder, 2.3-liter engines for the company's Pinto. Up to now, metric motors for this compact car have been imported from metric countries.

Caterpillar Tractor has a basic policy requiring parts and components manufactured anywhere in the world to be interchangeable. Regardless of national legislation, or the lack of it, the company has begun to phase out the inch–pound system by designing new products to metric measurements and ISO standards, where they have been established. Deere & Company and International Harvester are likewise beginning the switch to metric for new products. Deere has made a special study of costs and found that they are likely to amount to $1 million a year if spread over a ten-year changeover period, but hundreds of millions of dollars if attempted in a single year. The main difference is that during the gradual conversion that is contemplated virtually no machine tools will have to be replaced; they can either be converted inexpensively or allowed to wear out, whereupon new, metric machine tools will be bought.

Honeywell, which has been manufacturing to metric standards and dimensions abroad and to inches and pounds for the U.S. market, is also beginning a gradual shift to wholly metric production. Lowell Foster, Honeywell's director of corporate standardization, believes many companies that have not carefully studied conversion are greatly exaggerating anticipated expenses. "Actually, we have found the costs quite nominal," he says.

IBM'S CONVERSION PLAN

If one had to pick a single case study of a thoroughly planned and executed company metrication program, IBM's would be the natural choice. IBM began earliest and is proceeding most rapidly. By 1976, engineering and manufacturing will reflect a general companywide preference for metric measurements and standards, and two years later all new product designs will conform to metric standards, except in special cases where the use of metric would be decidedly uneconomical.

As early as 1964, IBM became "bilingual" to the extent that engineering diagrams and other technical documents quoted measurements in both metric and nonmetric units. This so-called dual-dimensioning is common practice among multinational firms. It is also a nuisance, for it adds to costs and sometimes causes confusion and errors.

Two years later a corporate team was formed to make a continuing study of the feasibility of switching entirely to metric. After weighing the pros and cons annually, the team concluded in 1971 that the time was ripe to begin total conversion.

IBM's approach stresses the adoption of a general strategy rather than a rigid program, and that strategy closely parallels Branscomb's rule of reason. In fact, explains L. John Rankine, corporate standards director, "We view metrication as a series of individual business decisions—literally hundreds of them—each made on its own merits. When the day comes when we find outselves paying a premium for, say, drafting paper or sheet steel with 'customary' dimensions, we'll switch to a standard metric size. We'll have to run with the tide—maybe even ahead in places, but not so far ahead that we pay penalties for having things made especially to order just for the sake of being metric."

EASIER THAN EXPECTED

As it emerges from the planning stage, IBM's metric program is going even more smoothly than the men in charge expected. In addition to employees, regular suppliers of parts and materials are kept informed of the program. "We'll work out problems with them as we would with any new technology or process," says Adrian G. Weaver, director of internal standards practice and head of the firm's Metric Panel.

Within the company the reaction has been overwhelmingly favorable, especially from technical people and those involved in world trade. In fact, the only common complaint is that IBM may not be moving far enough and fast enough. Internal education has proved to be no problem.

In some respects, IBM has inherently easier problems than most other large companies. The technologies of computers, copying machines, and most of its other products are changing so rapidly that tools, processes, and training are continually being replaced or revised anyway. Moreover, for most of its products, the company furnishes replacement parts and performs maintenance. In almost no case does the customer need to be concerned about measurement details. And so far IBM has found the cost of stocking dual inventories of metric and nonmetric parts to be minimal.

But IBM will continue indefinitely to use ½-inch magnetic tape for storing information, because to change this dimension would be to destroy the value of mountains of records stored on tape. "However, internally we may specify it as 12.7 millimeter tape," says John Rankine. "And if we introduce entirely new ways of storing information, the new components will conform to metric standards."

The company has not had to hire extra personnel to direct its conversion; instead, certain people in IBM's many divisions and departments have been assigned responsibility for carrying out various phases. All in all, Philip A. Markstrom, a standards expert who has been designated metric program manager, is far more at ease with metrication than he was a year ago, when companywide coordination appeared to be a formidable task.

5
Smoothing the
Road to Metric

This survey report assumes, perhaps rashly, that within a year or two Congress will pass legislation to make the metric system the nation's most-used system of weights and measures. The several bills now under consideration are so similar that, granting one will be passed, it is now possible to map the U.S. path to metric. There are already many clues as to what problems the United States will encounter, as well as what opportunities will arise from metrication. These clues come mainly from the experiences of firms that have already begun to go metric and from countries that have recently adopted national metric programs.

The current climate of opinion in the United States strongly favors the basic plan recommended by the U.S. Metric Study. Participation will be voluntary: individuals, firms, even whole industries may choose to stick primarily to inches and pounds well past the target date of ten years. Those who do participate will be aided by a national advisory board. This body will have no powers to compel compliance, but rather will act as a clearinghouse for information and will help coordinate plans. It will be the servant of U.S. metrication, not its master.

There is also considerable support for a much greater degree of compulsion. The Senate metric bill passed in 1972 provided that federal government agencies specify metric in their procurement soon after the initial planning phase ended. Proponents of the gradual, voluntary road to metric objected strongly to this provision. John Rankine of IBM, for one, feels compulsion is unnecessary. He explains, philosophically, that a voluntary program would inevitably "generate some degree of compulsion," especially during the later stages, when companies converting more slowly than their customers and suppliers would be under economic pressure to hasten. And, Rankine continues, government procurement mandates, such as were included in the Senate bill, could not be strictly enforced. Premature orders for uncommon metric parts and machines could not be filled, except at exorbitant prices.

THE EASE OF "SOFT" CONVERSION

What does "going metric" really mean to those involved? A great many current discussions are muddied by a basic lack of understanding of this point—specifically, a failure to distinguish between "soft" and "hard" conversion (i.e., between changing measurement language and changing machinery). Soft conversion is simply a matter of translation and relatively painless. For example, a dimension previously described as "one inch" is relabeled with the exact metric equivalent: "2.54 centimeters." Many manufacturing firms have already passed through this stage by dual-dimensioning. That is to say, their specifications and engineering drawings include both metric weights and measures and their nonmetric equivalents. Some packaged goods in food stores are labeled in pounds and ounces and also in grams.

In 1970 the National Aeronautics and Space Administration became the first government agency to carry out a thorough soft conversion. All of NASA's reports and other technical documents are being written in metric terms, although in many cases inch–pound standards still prevail. Nevertheless, soft conversion has proved a fairly effective way to encourage people to recognize metric measurements and even to think in metric terms.

Soft conversion is all that will be required for many years in many walks of life and even in some technically oriented jobs. The truth is that most people are never seriously concerned with precise measurements, much less with engineering standards. A cook who continues to use a quart of milk instead of a liter will not go far wrong; the difference is only 5%. And even much larger disparities are tolerable. Cake mixes that call for "two eggs" are basically insensitive to accuracy of measurement, for one jumbo egg is two-thirds bigger than a small egg.

THE REAL PROBLEMS— AND THE PHANTOM ONES

In manufacturing industries, many gauges are go, no go. The engineer who designs and specifies such an instrument has to worry about its dimensions, but the worker who uses it need only judge whether a part is too big or too small. A few real estate men have been disturbed by the prospect of remeasuring buildings and rewriting deeds by the millions. This turns out, on analysis, to be a phantom problem in any conversion program based on the rule of reason. Translation to metric would be made only when a new building is erected or when land is re-divided for sale and needs to be resurveyed. As a matter of fact, in some parts of the United States old deeds still contain ancient Spanish and French measurement units.

The crucial problems will arise following the preliminary period of soft conversion. A nation intent on becoming primarily metric must eventually embark on a wholesale program of hard conversions. This will to some extent affect everyone. Food will be sold by the kilogram instead of the pound. Parts used in manufacturing will be specified in conveniently round numbers of millimeters and centimeters. Building codes and industrial standards will have to be revised to accommodate materials available only in metric dimensions.

28

Some foresee enormous expense and confusion during this period of hard transition. In testimony before the House Science and Astronautics Committee in 1973, a spokesman for the American Iron and Steel Institute granted that soft conversion would be almost painless. But hard conversion, he said, is another story.

> This would involve physically changing all our products to round-number metric dimensions. . . . We would be faced with the massive task of retooling to produce these new products. . . . In addition, we would have to maintain very expensive inventories of both inch and metric products during the conversion period. And for some products, we would have to maintain dual inventories for decades, since inch products would have to be made as replacement parts for existing machines and systems.

> We might view the prospect of metric conversion with less alarm if we could expect to derive some benefit from it. Our studies show, however, that there would be little benefit. We sell more than 95 percent of our products in the United States and Canada. Metric conversion would merely increase our costs of serving this market. And of course foreign steel producers would have lower costs in serving this market, further worsening our trade deficit.

Those U.S. firms which have already begun metrication on their own obviously expect potential benefits to outweigh the costs of conversion during the transition period. And so do some observers whose companies are not yet ready to shift to metric. One is D. R. Burke, head of the standards and materials engineering department at Bell Telephone Laboratories. With virtually all its sales and manufacturing geared to U.S. markets, the Bell System has no intention of going metric before a national program is launched. Nevertheless, Burke has studied the problem as a leader of an ANSI metric advisory committee, and he foresees that the benefits of metrication will far outweigh transitional cost and inconveniences. In a recent speech, he outlined some major advantages of conversion:

A CHANCE FOR SPRING CLEANING

> Metrication offers an opportunity to rethink tolerances, and from doing so it may well be found that production time has been wasted in the past by maintaining a precision which was never warranted. Computers will reduce much of the work that would be involved in translating one measurement language to another, as will numerically controlled machine tools, which are increasingly being used in manufacture . . . .

> In general terms, it could be said that getting people to think metric makes them think about other things as well. It should generate a sort of spring cleaning that will make people look at existing practices and realize how many have accumulated just by habit and indifference, and how many can be effectively scrapped in the interest of efficiency.

> The room for improvement is enormous. For example, one large company expects to reduce its range of fasteners from 405 sizes to under 200. Another company will replace more than 280 types of customary size ball-bearing races with thirty metric types. What we are talking about is the opportunity which going metric gives to eliminate wasteful duplication in design and manufacture. . . . As Lord Ritchie-Calder, chairman of Britain's Metrication Board, has stated: "Industry is being made not only to think metric, but to think again."

29

A few concrete examples of independently conceived and executed programs indicate that metrication can produce substantial net benefits even without a coordinated program. Back in the 1950s the major drug companies changed the weights and volumes of many of their products to metric units. Costs were generally much less than anticipated. Retraining workers was no problem at all. Measuring devices and process machinery were easily modified. Pharmacists and physicians, already familiar with metric units, had little trouble adjusting the way they wrote and filled prescriptions. Each firm converted at its own pace. One of the largest made the transition in one year; a competitor took twice as long. Both feel now they could have moved faster without any disruption or confusion.

Similarly, many U.S. manufacturers of tapered roller bearings have been designing their new products to metric standard sizes. Here again costs and inconvenience have been minimal, and some companies are confident that the change will benefit their exports.

As an example of the "spring cleaning" to which Burke referred, the Industrial Fasteners Institute (sponsored by ANSI) has made a study of threaded fasteners (screws and bolts). At present, the world uses more than 110 combinations of standard threads and diameters—roughly half of them metric, the other half inch-based. The study showed, however, that most of these are superfluous. All could be replaced by a new assortment of just 25 threaded fasteners. Since the new range of fasteners is all metric, there is hope that it will eventually be adopted as a world standard by the International Standards Organization.

| MEETING THE PROBLEMS OF CONVERSION | Most companies will find that the problems of metric conversion are both internal and external, and that frequently one set will impinge on the other. It is the internal problems, however, that a company can—and often must—do something about, and prepare for. It is not that the external problems will take care of themselves; it is just that they are likely to come with more advance warning, and will often be solved through the action of outside forces or through joint efforts (e.g., by trade associations). |

Most of the internal problems that companies anticipate with regard to metric conversion revolve around two factors: costs and confusion. Judging from the experiences of those who have already undertaken to convert all or part of their operations, neither problem need be as large or as forbidding as it seems.

Production was the functional area in which most respondents to our survey looked for trouble, with 66% anticipating difficulties with conversion there. Next came purchasing, 48%; design, 48%; and maintenance, 46%. The percentages then dropped off sharply for other areas; 25% expected trouble in sales and marketing, 22% in clerical, 13% in executive management, 10% in packaging, 8% in finance, 5% in distribution, and 3% in legal. Respondents also made some scattered mentions of other potential problem areas, ranging from engineering land surveys to difficulties in truck repair shops.

In actuality, the problems encountered appear to be minimal. Among 470 respondents who said they used both metric and inch-pound measurement systems, most had experienced few or no interplant or interdepartmental problems arising from the use of dual measurement systems. A total of 202 (43%) said they had experienced no problems to speak of, and another 43% said these problems were minimal; 12% reported moderate problems, and only 2% reported great problems.

Obviously, for many companies the great stumbling block is the prospect of higher costs—particularly at a time when business is confronted with added costs for environmental measures, occupational health and safety, and minority-group employment and training. A two-year study by the American Iron and Steel Institute estimated that "hard conversion" of the steel industry (i.e., converting the industry's equipment to work in the metric system, rather than just changing the units of measurement) would cost in excess of $2 billion. This would include $758 million for advance preparation and $1,376 million for conversion (mainly for carrying dual inventories) over a ten-year period. Not included are the costs of unanticipated developments or of conversion in the mining, transport, and fabricating industries, all of which would be reflected in finished product prices.

The cost of metric conversion, and the extent of eventual benefits, are naturally matters of primary concern. Certainly expert planning and coordination can do a great deal to reduce confusion, conflicts, and the transitional expense of carrying dual inventories. But total costs are indeed difficult to estimate with any degree of certainty. During the U.S. Metric Study, for example, more than 100 firms submitted special cost studies. As mentioned earlier, cost estimated by firms that were roughly equivalent in size and type of business differed by a ratio of 10:1 or more.

Some feel that costs will be manageable, even in the short run, and that advance costing is bound to be unrealistic. "Any company that does a cost analysis in advance is just incurring an additional and needless cost," says Malcolm E. O'Hagan, executive director of ANSI's American National Metric Council.

IBM's John Rankine is of the same opinion. He does not believe that such forecasts are even worth attempting. "I'm afraid I'm a skeptic on the subject of cost," said Rankine in a talk to the National Association of Manufacturers. "I find costs very much influenced by management attitudes, and where the management attitude is 'let's go,' the cost of going metric is minimal. Where the management attitude is very negative, the costs tend to be very high. I really don't think anyone knows the cost of our total plan. The challenge is to find the minimum cost path in each significant decision area."

IBM's Philip Markstrom explained that the company first made the decision that the time had come to move to the metric system on a well-paced evolutionary basis. The next task was to find the most practical (i.e., realistic, least-cost) way to reach the objective. Like any problem, IBM executives felt, this one simply required an optimized solution.

Since the total accounting costs and presumed benefits appeared difficult, if not impossible, to implement, IBM is using an approach of controlled costs, with profit and loss being the control. As with a new product or device, each program manager has a budget, and it is his responsibility to achieve the desired end on time and within that budget. In the course of IBM's planning, it soon became evident that projected costs were too high in many cases and even imaginary in some. A program analysis also revealed that no special accounting practices were needed to allow for extraordinary first-product or process-design costs.

Deere & Company, in switching to metric, has found that virtually no machine tools have to be replaced, that items can be produced to either customary or metric measurement through conversion charts or dual dimensioned drawings, and that changing machine parts or scales is far less costly than replacing the entire tool. IBM's Markstrom comments dryly, "Most machines don't know what an inch is, and have to be told."

SPEAKING THE SAME LANGUAGE

The great advantage of using metric measurement, most advocates agree, is standardization. For multinational companies this means speaking a standardized international language. The problem frequently becomes: Which standard to use? There are many metric systems—SI, CGS, MKS, for example—and a great accumulation of metric data. Metal gauge (thickness), for instance, has different standards, with different tolerances. Which is truly an international standard?

Many companies for which standards are important urge the use of internationally agreed standards under SI. They are getting away from such terms as "gauge," and instead are specifying dimensional units—thicknesses plus tolerances.

There are other problems with metric. Is the word "metre" or is it "meter"? (To most Europeans a metre is a measurement and a meter is a measuring device, e.g., a voltmeter.) Is temperature to be given in Centigrade (which to a Frenchman means a degree of angle), in Kelvin (which involves numbers so large only a physicist could love them), or in Celsius? Are there commas or spaces between numerical triads (that is, is it 1,000,000 or 1 000 000?), and is a period or a comma to be used for the decimal marker? To simplify world communication, international standards must be set for all these things. When agreed standards already exist, any company is well advised to make them its own.

To minimize confusion in all these matters, the two key words are timing and communication. Timing is a matter of both when a company should start doing what it has decided to do, and in what sequence things should be done. Communication involves not only employee awareness and education, but also uniform definition of terms, quantities, and conversion constants.

AWARENESS FOR SOME, EDUCATION FOR OTHERS

Awareness and education are separate processes and should be carried on separately. Awareness involves orienting all personnel—production and research people, middle management, top management—with regard to metric conversion before it begins and while it is taking place. Education, on the other hand, should be addressed primarily to the people who will work with metrics. They should be educated only to the degree that they need it. For example, inch-oriented workers should become proficient in converting metric measurements to inches and vice versa, while design people should become adept at thinking in metric units.

WHAT IS A WATT?

The common electrical measures—amperes, ohms, volts, and watts—are units created specifically for the metric system. They have been so completely absorbed into our customary system, however, that a great many people believe volts, watts, and amperes *are* customary measures.

The common link between electrical measurements and mechanical measurements is the watt, which in the metric system is a unit of both electrical and mechanical power. This can be shown by a set of formulas involving various units. The definitions used are: velocity = distance per unit of time; acceleration = velocity per unit of time; force = mass times acceleration; work (or energy) = force times distance; and power = work per unit of time. These are the equations in metric units:

Velocity $V = m/s$

Acceleration $A = (m/s) \div s = m/s^2$

Force $1 \text{ newton} = kg(m/s^2)$

Work $1 \text{ joule} = kg(m/s^2)(m) = kg(m^2/s^2)$

Power $1 \text{ watt} = kg(m^2/s^2) \div s = kg(m^2/s^3)$

where m designates distance (in meters); s equals time (in seconds); and kg equals mass (in kilograms).

Now amperes, ohms, and volts are derived. Two of the most basic electrical equations are $E = IR$ (electrical potential equals current times resistance) and $P = EI$ (electrical power equals potential times current). Translated into units:

$E = IR$ volts = amperes × ohms

$P = EI$ watts = volts × amperes

Thus in the metric system it is possible to build a coherent system of simple formulas in which the watt equals a unit of mechanical power. The same thing cannot be done in the customary system, where the unit for force is commonly deemed to be a foot-pound per second and the unit of power is the horsepower, which is 550 foot-pounds per second. Here the equations for velocity, acceleration, force, work, and power are complicated by conversion factors. To make the system coherent—i.e., to make the units come out right—certain special units have been created, such as the poundal (one pound times one foot per second squared) as a unit of force, and the foot poundal per second (one pound times one foot squared per second cubed) as a unit of power.

The poundal is rarely used in practice, and most engineers regard the horsepower as a cumbersome anachronism. It is still quite commonly used to describe the capability of an internal combustion engine. But for the electrical car, the metric system can describe capabilities directly: Moving a mass of so many kilograms over so many meters should require so many watts.

Not only does the customary system lack coherence, but some of its units are not fixed and absolute. One old aphorism of the customary system says that "a pint's a pound the world around." Yet a pound is not a pound the world around. Since a pound reflects the attraction of gravity—which may vary with altitude, latitude, and air pressure—it is not the same at the equator as in the temperate zones, not the same on a mountaintop as at the seashore, not the same in a thunderstorm as on a clear, sunny day. A kilogram, however, is a unit of mass, not weight—so a kilogram is a kilogram wherever you find it, in or out of this world.

Because of the great interdependence of all operations in most companies, it is important to make sure that all components go metric before the end result is supposed to be metric. Everyone doesn't have to start on a new system at the same time, but the right people have to be doing the right thing at the right time. Many companies believe in following the British pattern in education—teach the technician just what he needs to know and just before he has to use it. Too much too soon can be as bad as too little too late.

Most respondents to our survey had apparently done little thinking about the matter of educating employees. Seven percent of those responding said their company had plans for metric education; 3% had such a program already in effect. But 61% had no plans at all, and the other 29% were uncertain about whether their firms had such plans.

It is in the area of education that respondents feel they need the most help: 59% said they could use assistance with employee training methods in the event of nationwide conversion. Almost as many—53%—showed interest in getting help with reference to subsidies or tax relief, 31% with reference to industry coordinating boards, 29% with reference to explaining conversion to customers and suppliers, and 23% with reference to relaxation of such legal standards as building codes. Respondents also cited a large number of miscellaneous areas in which they felt help was needed, such as conversion of machinery and labeling of consumer products.

CUSTOMER AND SUPPLIER PROBLEMS

Once a company recognizes its need for help with internal problems, the chances are good that it has started on the road toward keeping down metric conversion costs. Respondents to the survey did predict that more metric conversion programs would arise in internally oriented functional areas (as already noted, 66% expected problems in production, 48% in design, 46% in maintenance) than in functional areas with strong external links (48% in purchasing, 25% in marketing and sales). Nevertheless, many showed a nagging worry about external problems over which they had little or no control.

Many were concerned about problems they might have with suppliers; a smaller number had similar misgivings about customers. Assuming a national conversion to the metric system, 63% answered that they expected problems with suppliers' difficulty in converting and in measurement errors in goods they bought, while 60% believed they would have extra costs because of suppliers' conversion problems. Forty-five percent expected to have problems with mixed metric and inch-pound orders for customers. Relatively few (about 20%) expected problems with suppliers' refusal to fill metric shipments or customers' refusal to accept metric shipments.

So far it appears that few of these problems have reared their ugly heads. Of the responding firms that now use both measurement systems, 43% have experienced no problems with customers or suppliers, 45% have had minimal problems, 11% reported they have had moderate problems, and only 1% have had great problems.

The explanation for this may well be that a well-thought-out company conversion is practically unnoticeable to customers and suppliers. Equipment built entirely of metric parts can still be used to make inch-based products. Functional design and performance are always more important than the measurement system used to describe the function.

The businesses surveyed, whether they oppose metric conversion or profess no qualms over it, have in common an overriding concern with antitrust implications. John P. Roche, president of the American Iron and Steel Institute, has pointed out that much cooperation, coordination, and joint planning will be needed among producers, suppliers, and purchasers in order to bring about an efficient transition to the metric system. If a group of companies were to agree, for example, on a specific date after which they would buy only metric fasteners, how could they avoid antitrust prosecution and triple-damage suits by nonmetric manufacturers? Without some measures to eliminate or reduce their jeopardy, the maximum degree of coordination is not likely to take place.

Perhaps the agency best suited to develop such agreements is the American National Standards Institute; it is the natural choice to serve as a trade association while the manufacturing industry is converting. ANSI has studied the antitrust problem in depth, reporting in 1971:

> Since new engineering standards must be developed and promulgated before any meaningful progress toward metric conversion could be accomplished, any nationally coordinated . . . program that contains . . . time limits would result in engineering standards development *crash programs*. . . .

> It would seem that not only would individual companies be exposed to considerable antitrust risks, but the standardization bodies themselves could also become parties to any litigation which might develop. . . .

Thus ANSI supports the type of voluntary program described in both the House and Senate bills.

A number of businessmen also profess some concern on behalf of their ultimate customers—the public. "How about the user's point of view?" asked one. "The homeowner's burden cannot be absorbed by tax relief or increased prices. . . . There is an extremely large inventory of inch-pound devices owned by the ultimate user—the citizen!"

Yet most people have already had considerable contact with metric measurements without giving them a second thought—in photographic film, prescription drugs, electrical equipment and light bulbs, Olympic swimming pools, skis, bicycles, and even metric measuring cups to go with European cookbooks. The National Bureau of Standards points out that the trend toward packaged goods (now 90% of all foods sold) "has eliminated most of the confusion that a metric changeover would impose on the consumer." And it is a rare auto mechanic who does not possess metric tools, since they are required by more than a quarter of the cars on America's highways today.

For other areas, a program of broad public education would seem to offer the ideal solution. Most schoolchildren are already being taught something about metric measurement, and in some school systems and states the subject is compulsory.

As noted earlier, Australia has eased the transition to metric more successfully than Great Britain by paying greater heed to education of the general public. Major horse races in Australia are over metric distances, a real triumph for metric considering that this is a sport of hidebound traditionalists. Chances are that most people were never quite sure how long a furlong was anyway.

A few small companies are already profiting by switching part of their production to metric—by manufacturing at least those metric tools and devices that the public and other businesses will undoubtedly want and need. A spokesman for Thorsen Tool Company of Dallas foresees a growing market, even without congressional action: "Within four or five years, every mechanic in the United States will have both metric and customary wrenches in his toolbox." And Kenyon Taylor, president of Regal Beloit, points out that metric conversion is already well under way as far as his company is concerned. Its sales of special tools and gauges (and even bathroom scales) were 4% metric in 1972, climbed to about 10% in 1973, and will be almost 20% in 1974.

There is probably room for only a limited number of firms to make hay by getting metric products on the market early. But the fact that it is happening at all is indicative that the problem of metric vis-à-vis the public may eventually be one not of being too far ahead, but of being too far behind.

THE INEVITABILITY OF METRIC CONVERSION

Whether the U.S. will join the ranks of metric nations is no longer doubtful; the only questions are *when* and *how.* The use of the metric system in this country is steadily increasing, partly because we trade in an almost exclusively metric world and partly because our native sciences and advanced technology are already predominantly metric.

If nature were allowed to take its course, with no national plan for conversion, the United States might be mainly metric by the year 2000, or perhaps two or three decades later. A coordinated national program would advance the date to 1985, or maybe a little earlier.

The results of this survey show that a substantial majority of U.S. management is in favor of deliberate conversion beginning soon. For several years now, this has been the position taken by associations representing scientists, engineers, and educators. This is hardly surprising, since they have a stake in the metric system. But now other organizations are joining the march to metrication. The usually conservative American Medical Association announced in January 1973 that its journals would henceforth use the metric system exclusively. And the National Association of Manufacturers, at a board of directors meeting in February 1973, released a statement which read in part: "The NAM believes that the long-term interests of the United States will best be served by adoption of the International System of Units (SI) and thus be in total harmony with the rest of the industrial and commercial world. The NAM further believes that industry should participate in and support the development of standards that may be required by such adoption."

The board of directors of the Chamber of Commerce of the United States had made its position clear even earlier. "The United States is steadily changing over to the international metric system of measurement. . . . The Chamber supports voluntary changeover to the international metric system of measurement as soon as practicable, and increased U.S. participation in international voluntary standards activities related thereto."

There is even some strong support from organizations that may find the transition to metric unusually difficult. In 1972 Carl A. Beck, representing the National Small Business Association, said at a Senate hearing:

> To say that small business is involved is the gross understatement of the year. Our company, for example, employs about 50 people and has annual sales approaching a million dollars. . . . Our best estimates in the U.S. Metric Study were that it might cost us as much as the amount of a full year's dollar volume of sales to completely convert to metric measurements. Even spread out over a ten-year period, this would be a substantial burden. Yet, in spite of this, we recognize it must be done, and the sooner the better.

A similar attitude was expressed by one of the respondents to the AMA survey, a manufacturer who declared: "We must bear the difficulties of this conversion period soon for our sons and daughters of the future. If we don't start soon, then this generation can be considered selfish and irresponsible."

Some of the respondents to the survey—and standards experts who were specially interviewed—spoke of metrication as an important step in keeping the United States in harmony with the rest of the world. Many were concerned with improving international standards, but others simply wanted a common, unambiguous measurement language that could be used by companies and even vacationing travelers throughout the world.

There was more disagreement on the question of what immediate effect metric conversion would have on U.S. trade, specifically on the balance of payments. Some pointed out, as did the American Iron and Steel Institute, that adoption of metric standards might open the United States to a flood of imports from nations that were already familiar with metric and could produce more cheaply.

But on the other side of the coin, many companies are worried that, with the British Commonwealth rushing to metric, it will become increasingly hard to export inch–pound products to countries where replacement parts may be scarce and where workmen will be unfamiliar with nonmetric measurements and unequipped with nonmetric tools. Also, the Common Market has begun a certification program that is like an underwriter's seal of approval. Products that meet Common Market standards, which are mainly metric, will be easily traded. Those that fail to meet the standards must be tested, and the cost and inconvenience of testing could be a trade barrier higher than any ordinary tariff. (One observer noted, however, that U.S. markets represent such a huge target for foreign manufacturers that they could afford to "tool up to produce in cubits and shekels, if those were the common U.S. measurement units.")

As another respondent to this survey pointed out: "The crux of the matter is not one of going to the metric language of measurement, but one of going to the full SI and to the associated standards that will be created in SI. . . . The cost of not going to SI is economic death for the U.S.A. in world markets over ten or twenty years."

Whatever action Congress takes with regard to a conversion program, it is clear that the nation should be better prepared for metrication than it is today. Two steps can be taken immediately. U.S. participation in international standards-making can be greatly augmented. And U.S. children, especially in primary schools, can be taught the metric system much more intensively as an alternate language of measurement. Sooner or later they are going to need it.